Sardinian Knot Stitch

Interpreted by Gioja Ralui

The authors

Gioja Ralui is a pseudonym composed of a few parts of our names. We are all traditional embroidery enthusiasts and none of us is an embroideress by profession or operates a school of embroidery. We met "virtually" many years ago, being members of a group born on the web where you could explore the various aspects of classic embroidery and exchange ideas, tips, information and news. Later we met "for real" and a true friendship was born! Each of us continued to embroider while the first blogs were started, thus Renata started writing tutorials on *punt'e nù* as she had learned it, while Jeanine and Luisa started experimenting with this technique. Then, during a trip to Italy, Jeanine and Giovanna visited Renata in Sardinia and then Giovanna too learned to embroider *punt'e nù*. From there came the idea to write this book which we hope will help to keep the interest in this traditional Sardinian embroidery alive.

Text: Renata

Photography: Renata, Jeanine, Rachel

Editing, typography and graphics: Jeanine

Coordination: Giovanna

Embroidery and patterns: Renata, Jeanine, Luisa, Giovanna

Acknowledgements

Without the help and support of numerous people this project would not have come to fruition, therefore we would like to thank Renata's embroidery teacher; Veronica for the photos of the Teulada (CA) costumes; Pina Monne and the town of Sennariolo (OR) for the magnificent mural on the cover and Yvette Stanton for her invaluable technical help in the creation of this book. Antonello Steri of the vacation village *Rosso porpora - Is Loccis Santus* (CI) for hosting us and consenting to the use of his premises as the setting for the photos of our embroideries (http://www.sardegnautentica.com/it/) and Maura Puddu for her collaboration in the relative photography. And finally we thank Luisa's husband who always helps and encourages her, even if he never knows what she's talking about! Giovanna's husband and son because they support "a woman crazy for embroidery" around the house! Rachel, Jeanine's daughter, for her help with photography, photo editing and retouching and for having patiently tolerated her mother who was always in front of the computer in her room!

A portion of the proceeds from book sales will be donated to charity for the children of the *Mission of Camp Garba*, Kenya.

Sardinian Knot Stitch

Interpreted by Gioja Ralui

Table of Contents

ITALY

Sardinia

Teulada

Introduction

The first time that I happened to observe a piece of punt'e nù embroidery up close I was stunned: it was a set of Altar linens for Mass composed of three pieces (corporal, lavabo towel and purificator) of white linen finely embroidered with meticulous stitching which was ever so slightly raised. But the most extraordinary thing was that, when I turned the pieces over, I could hardly distinguish the embroidery from the weave of the fabric.

The work intrigued me so much that right away I started to do some research into this mysterious embroidery technique. I was told that it was *Teulada stitch* and that the pieces had been embroidered by a lady from my town presumably around the 1930s. I had already heard talk of this *Teulada stitch* but I had never seen anything embroidered with it.

It was not easy to find someone to teach it to me, but in the end I met a kind and helpful lady, to whom I am deeply grateful, who accepted the task of becoming my teacher. Since then I have completed small projects, without any pretence of being an expert in this technique, attempting also to adapt it to daily necessities and modern tastes, besides that of my own personal taste and imagination, something which may make purists of the technique turn up their noses. Moreover, already in the past, as will be discussed later, there were changes in the intended use of this embroidery, precisely because of changing tastes and habits.

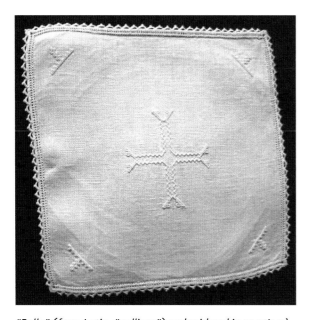

"Palla" (from Latin: "pallium") embroidered in punt'e nù.

Back side of the central cross motif.

Detail of the finishing for the edge.

With this book we intend only to give a small and modest demonstration of the beauty and possible applications of this embroidery technique of which the unsurpassed masters are the artisan embroiderers of Teulada. If you are planning a vacation in Sardinia, dedicate at least one day to visiting this town, its artisan activities and its splendid coastline: it is definitely worth the trouble!

* * *

In Sardinian it is called: *punt'e nù* (literal translation: knot stitch) and indeed the stitch is constructed of a knot. This technique is originally from a town in the extreme south of Sardinia, Teulada, and it is for this that it is also known as *Teulada stitch*. It is

Enlarged detail of the central cross.

difficult to trace its origins as until now there haven't been many written sources. The scholar Ovidio Addis, of Teuladan origins, refers to this fact in his work *Trilogia teuladina [Teuladan Trilogy]* as follows:

"[...The brothers also had the sad task of assisting those destined for the noose... The last hanged man is connected – tradition tells – to the origin of the Teulada stitch, the unusual embroidery of exceptional beauty and technique, known to the authors of folklore and handicrafts:

Ziu Antoni Salis fell in love with a lady and his ardor was so impetuous that not pitchforks, friars nor the halter of the noose could divert events or his destiny.

Traditional Sardinian loom.

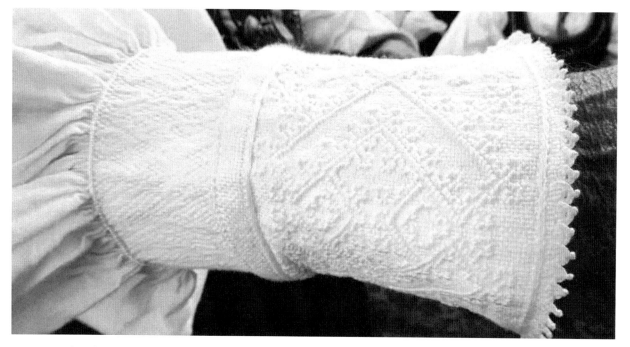
"Pungittu" (cuff) of the traditional male costume shirt of Teulada embroidered in punt'e nù.

In a night of love, the two lovers decided to "take out" the other, the husband of the lady. And so it happened and everything was discovered by an attentive justice official. Ziu Antoni passed his final night in Saint Francis praying and eating biscuits. The next day,

"Pibionis" (Sardinian raised weaving technique) tapestry.

Ceramic plate.

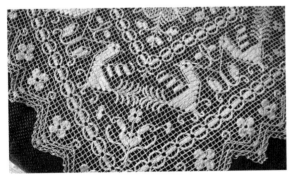

Tablecloth in Filet needle lace.

contrite, he ascended the scaffold and, devoutly – even his confessor said so – passed on. The lady, who was pregnant, and good for her, was sentenced to prison for life. In the boredom of her cell, she embroidered and embroidered; inventing the Teulada stitch and creating such a beautiful blanket that the baroness – having received it as a gift – pardoned her. She lived piously for many more years with the needle and the rosary in remembrance of her men, her sufferings, her sorrows...]"

Whatever its origins might be, *punt'e nù* was known to all the women of Teulada who, using linen fabric produced on looms, sewed men's traditional folk costumes, embroidering the collars (in Sardinian: tzughera) and the cuffs (in Sardinian: pungittusu). The traditional men's folk costume of Teulada is influenced by Spanish origins. Its

Armrest of a carved wooden bench.

characteristics are: the *sombrero* hat of grey felt (while for the most part, traditional costumes of the island use the *berritta*), and most of all the high, stiff collar of the shirt, densely embroidered with *punt'e nù* and bordered by a fine lace entirely made with the needle.

The motifs reproduced with this embroidery technique are strictly geometric and have profound symbolic meaning. Many of them occur frequently in other traditional Sardinian handicrafts like pottery, tapestries and rugs, hope chests and carved wooden chairs and in the works of filet lace (see some examples on pages 4 and 5).

Is denteddasa, the zig-zag, *is gruxittasa, sa prama, is caboniscus, su calixi picau, s'arenada, su cumpingiu, sa cerexia,* etc. are all motifs that are based on

ancient iconographic traditions, from those of the prehistoric Mediterranean world to the Semitic and Phoenician Punic and later Christian, Byzantine and Arabic (Quintina Culurgioni *Su punt'e nù e su punt'a brodu,* published by the Commune of

Bread for wedding celebrations.

Basket woven with figures in traditional costume.

Backboard of a carved wooden hope chest.

Ceramic jug.

Teulada). Doretta Davanzo Poli has written an interesting essay on the symbolic meanings of the iconographic motifs typical to traditional Sardinian handicrafts in *Tessuti – Tradizione e innovazione della tessitura in Sardegna [Fabrics – Tradition and the innovation of weaving in Sardinia]*, edited by Ilisso, found on the website: www.sardegnadigitallibrary.it (text in Italian).

Starting at the beginning of the 1900s, this embroidery technique was also being used on trousseau pieces, while the traditional men's costume was progressively abandoned, being substituted by more practical and functional garments. Currently *punt'e nù* is used mostly for ornamenting tablecloths, doilies, curtains and other trousseau items with motifs of finesse and unparalleled value.

"Tzughèra" (collar) of the traditional male costume of Teulada.

Materials

Materials for Sardinian Knot Stitch

Sardinian Knot Stitch uses *evenweave fabric (the same number of threads in warp and weft) and the threads used must be composed of twisted fibres like pearl cotton.*

For those who are stitching this embroidery for the first time, we would recommend a fabric that has easily visible fabric threads like the one pictured in **photo a** (28ct) so that you can clearly see where to execute the work. For practising, you can even use a more openly woven fabric (for example: 22ct or 25ct) using a thicker thread (for example: pearl cotton no. 8). With a 28ct fabric we recommend pearl cotton no. 12 as pictured in **photo b**.

A tapestry needle is preferable in order to avoid accidentally splitting the fabric threads.

photo a

photo b

Instructions

Working Sardinian Knot Stitch

Sardinian Knot Stitch is *worked on the vertical fabric threads (it doesn't matter whether they are warp or weft threads as long as the fabric is an evenweave).*

In **photo 1** the green arrows indicate the fabric threads on which to work the embroidery, while the red ones indicate those that are never to be used. During the working, the fabric is **never** turned (the work can only be turned upside-down if absolutely necessary – turned 180° – but never turned 90°; for example: if you are working along a border of a square piece of fabric, when you are finished one side, you **must not** rotate the fabric 90° in order to embroider the adjacent side, instead you must proceed vertically, keeping the fabric in the same position). The embroidery can be done in all four diagonal directions, that is:

• from top left towards bottom right or vice-versa,
• from bottom left towards top right or vice-versa.

The core of Sardinian Knot Stitch is a knot. According to the way in which they are placed, the knots form the most simple motifs: *sa dentedda* (the tooth), *is spronis* (the spurs), *sa gruxitta* (the cross: the "x", by convention, in Sardinian makes a sound which does not exist in the Italian alphabet, so it is not read as "cs" but like the French "j" of "jour"). To begin let's embroider a zig-zag motif, used commonly as a small border. The black dots indicate the position on the fabric where the knots should be placed in the zig-zag (**photo 2**). As you can see, each dot is on a vertical fabric thread which is where it should be worked, as indicated by the green arrows in **photo 1**. Slide the needle under the vertical fabric thread as in **photo 3**, leaving a "tail" of about 3 cm which will be secured under the next

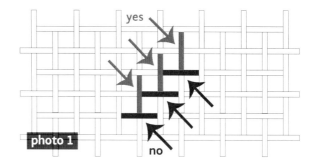

photo 1

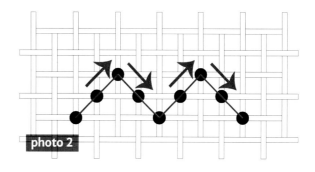

photo 2

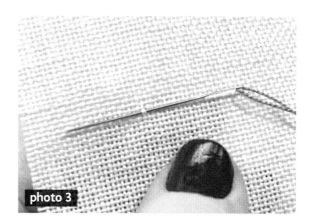

photo 3

two knots. Slide the needle again under the same vertical fabric thread to form the knot by placing the working thread over the needle as shown (**photos 4** and **5**). Slide the needle under the next vertical fabric thread that is to the right but one row higher, see **photo 6**) and make another knot (see **photo 7**), catching the "tail", left suspended at the beginning, inside the knot. After another 3 or 4 knots, you can cut away the "tail" which is by now secured (**photo 8**). In the event that you embroider a "closed" motif, one where your last stitch is where you began, you can start the work by "skipping" the

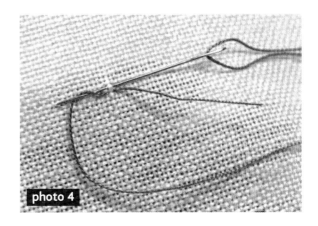

photo 4

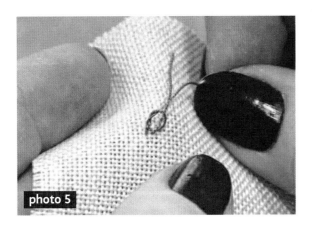

photo 5

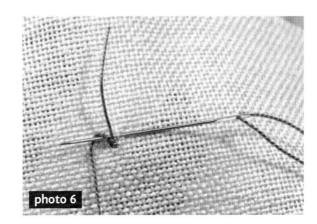

photo 6

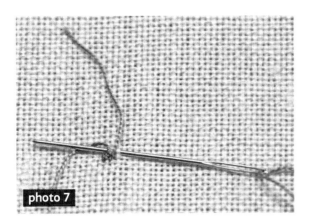

photo 7

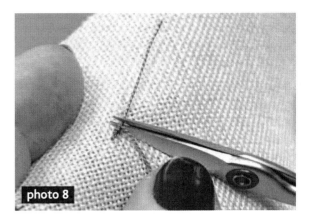

photo 8

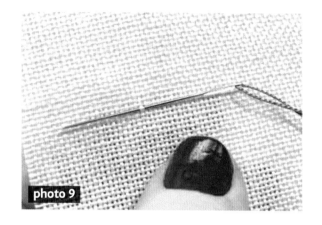

photo 9

first knot, thereby ensuring the uniformity of the work. Once you have passed the working thread under the first vertical fabric thread (**photo 9**), slide the needle under the next fabric thread to the right but one row higher (**photo 10**) and make the knot (**photos 11** and **12**). In this way, the first knot is "skipped" and will then be executed as the last knot when the motif is "closed" by returning to the starting point (**photo 13**). Insert the tip of the needle just to the right of the last knot executed and pull it through to the back side of the work, securing the working thread end according to **photos 20** and **21**.

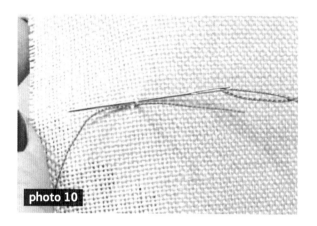

photo 10

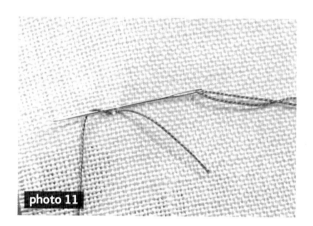

photo 11

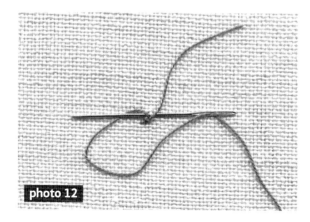

photo 12

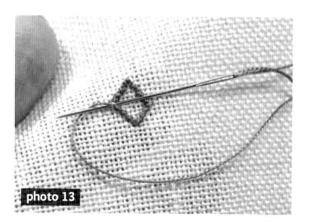

photo 13

How to hold the thread: ascending

When ascending, the working thread is held towards the bottom of the work: this allows better vision of the vertical fabric thread to be worked with the needle (**photo 14**). The working thread is placed up and over the needle as indicated in **photo 15**.

How to hold the thread: descending

When descending, the working thread is held above the needle and the fabric thread to be worked, as you can see in **photo 16**. The working thread is then passed down and under the needle as indicated in **photo 17**.

Working not on the diagonal

In a few cases, it is possible to work in horizontal or vertical directions rather than on the diagonal, but it is better to do so only for small sections as the effect is not very pleasing. If you must do a long section, it is better to execute a zig-zag of a single row of knots (eg. one knot up and one knot down if working horizontally or one to the left and one to the right if working vertically, see the first pattern on page 17). In a few motifs there are some parts that you can embroider vertically as

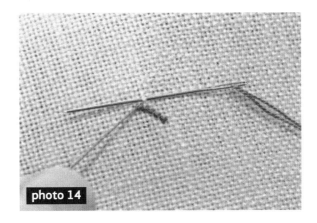

photo 14

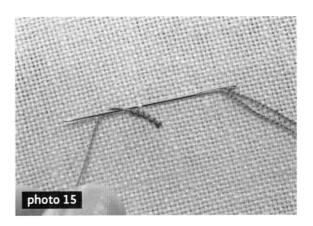

photo 15

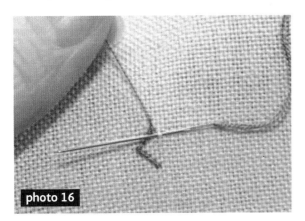

photo 16

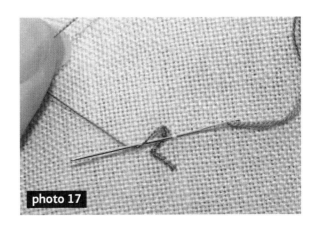

photo 17

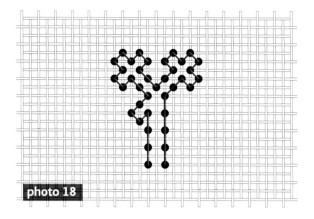

photo 18

photo 19

in the *sa prama* (the palm), where the stem is realized in vertical stitches, or (**photos 18** and **19**) the neck of *su caboniscu* (the cockerel). In this case, you must skip a row of fabric threads in order to find the next vertical one in the same line to be worked. Because of this, the knots are slightly farther apart.

How to secure the thread end when finishing the work or at the end of a "closed" motif

Bring the working thread to the back side of the work by inserting the needle just above and to the right of (if ascending), or below (if descending) the knot, then on the back side pass the needle under the last 3 or 4 already made knots (**photos 20** and **21**). You may wish to change to a sharp-tipped needle for this step.

How to secure the thread end and start a new one

If you must change your working thread to continue the work, the two working threads, the one ending and the one beginning, are hidden together in the next few knots made with the new thread, the same as when you begin a new working thread at the beginning of the work (**photos 4** to **7**).

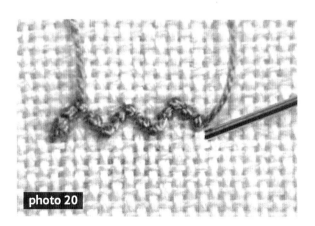

photo 20

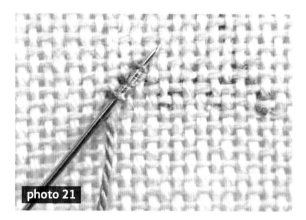

photo 21

The layout of the work and the corners

The embroideries done in Sardinian Knot Stitch are stitched in bands of one or more motifs (*arenada* [the pomegranate], *caboniscu* [the cockerel], *arrosa* [the rose], *cadira* [the chair], etc.) that are repeated in sequences. Organizing the work requires attention to ensure that the design remains decentralized. Counting the threads allows you to determine how many times the motif can be repeated in the available space, leaving equal distance on all sides and between the embroidery and the hem of the fabric. The centre of each band and the corners require particular attention: the motifs in these places must become "reflected" at 90° horizontally for the centre of the lateral band and at 45° for the corner.

photo 22

The following are a few photos (**22-24**) which illustrate the "reflected" corners. Sometimes in the corner, it can be necessary to fill in the gaps which are formed by the "reflected" motifs. In this case, you can insert small filling motifs (*prenimentu*) like the cross in the corner of **photo 25** for example.

photo 23

photo 24

photo 25

photo 26

The hems

Tablecloths and napkins embroidered with Sardinian Knot Stitch are usually finished with narrow hems of a maximum width of a few centimetres secured with a simple hem stitch (**photo 26**), or a four-sided stitch (**photo 27**), or a simple Peahole hem stitch. Other times the decoration, aside from the drawn thread work which is always present, is enriched with a scalloped edge formed by buttonhole stitch arcs, simple (**photo 28**) or with a picot (**photo 29**), or more complex as shown in **photo 30**.

photo 27

photo 28

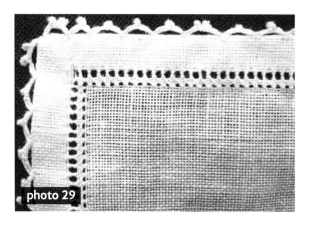

photo 29

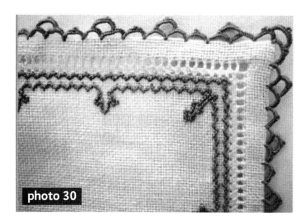

photo 30

Patterns

The Borders

The motifs and borders *of Sardinian Knot Stitch are made up of designs handed down by tradition and are similar to those which are found in other forms of Sardinian handicrafts.*

The geometric motifs are repeated and alternated and are often finished by a more or less elaborated frame of simple figures: the final result depends on the available space and on the individual taste of the embroiderer. We offer a few border designs with their names in Sardinian and English and photos at actual size. We start with one of the more simple borders, the zig-zag single line, only 2 stitches high. We arrive at the end with the more complex, the last border has a height of 22 stitches.

su zig-zag • the zig-zag

design height: 2 stitches, start where indicated by the arrow

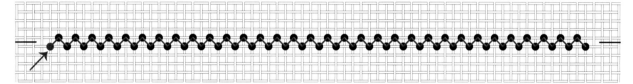

su zig-zag • the zig-zag

design height: 4 stitches, start where indicated by the arrows

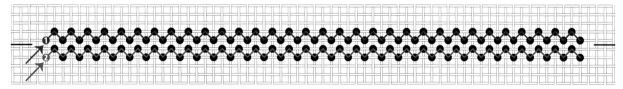

is gruxittasa • the crosses

design height: 11 stitches, start where indicated by the arrow

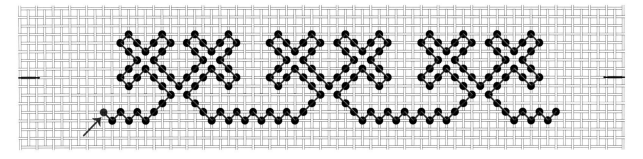

is gruxittasa • the crosses

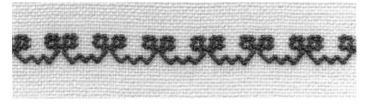

design height: 9 stitches, start where indicated by the arrow

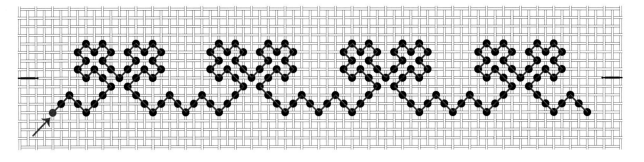

is denteddasa • the teeth

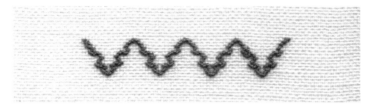

design height: 13 stitches, start where indicated by the arrow

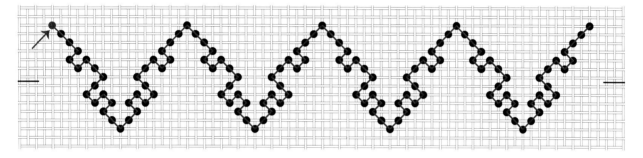

is denteddasa • the teeth

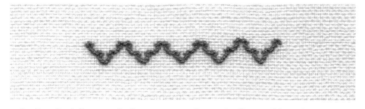

design height: 8 stitches, start where indicated by the arrow

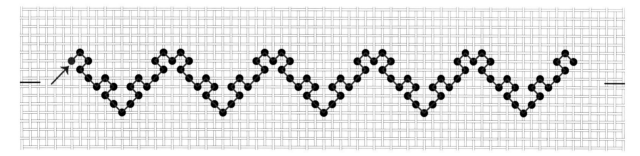

is follittasa • the little leaves

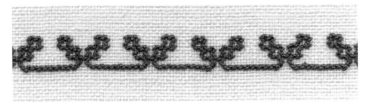

design height: 11 stitches, start where indicated by the arrow

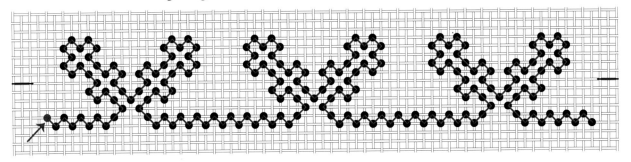

is follittasa • the little leaves

design height: 14 stitches, start where indicated by the arrow

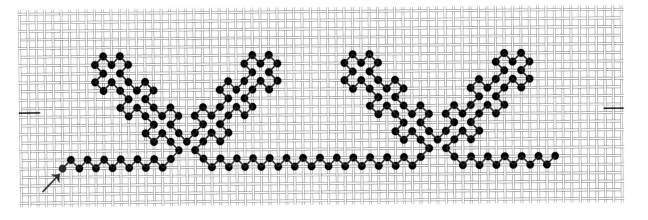

is spronis • the spurs

design height: 7 stitches, start where indicated by the arrow

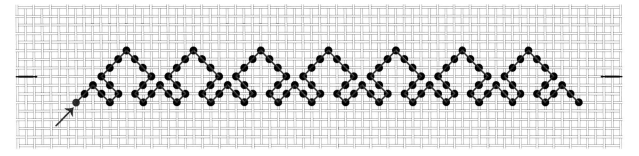

su coru • the heart

design height: 22 stitches, start where indicated by the arrows

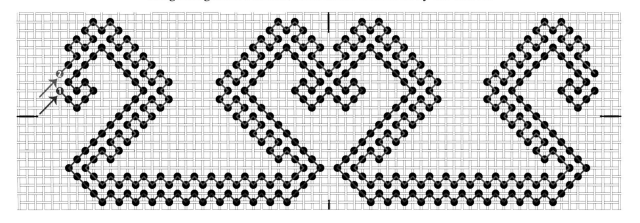

Patterns

The Motifs

The motifs and borders *of Sardinian Knot Stitch are made up of designs handed down by tradition and are similar to those which are found in other forms of Sardinian handicrafts. They are strictly geometric and, starting with the knot (su nu), simple figures are formed which repeat and alternate (su sterrimentu – the framework), and are completed by other figures (su prenimentu – the fillings or embellishments). The final result is determined by the space available and by the individual taste of the embroiderer.*

The simple figures (eg. *sa cerexia, su calixi picau*) can change in dimension while the embellishment figures (eg. *su caboniscu, sa menduledda, su cuadrifoliu, sa prama, su cumpingiu*) can also change in their depiction (eg.: *su caboniscu* can be embroidered by itself or in groups of two, evenly spaced or reflected). We offer a few designs with the names in Sardinian and English and the photos are at actual size. It is necessary to emphasize that the classification that follows is a guideline, traditionally a few motifs are used in more than one way. *Su caboniscu*, for example, especially as a couple, is a "framework" figure which is repeated along the side and forms the backbone of an embroidered band, however those smaller ones (see the photo on page 28) can serve as "filling or embellishment" to fill an empty rhombic space which is formed, for example, between two adjoining pomegranate "framework" motifs. Sometimes, for reasons of space and continuity, we have had to show only a portion of the pattern. In these cases we have provided one quarter or one half, but only when it was unavoidable and these are to be repeated as mirror images. Rarely, and only to show the entire motif for indicating the execution order of the embroidery, we have omitted the background fabric representation to simplify the pattern and to make it easier to follow. Always start the embroidery on a vertical fabric thread.

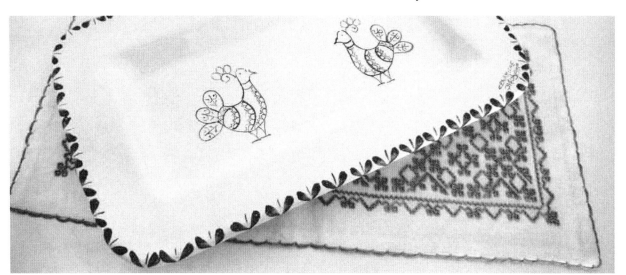

A few examples of "de sterrimentu" (framework) motifs

s'arrosa • the rose

width of *complete* design: 81 stitches, height of *complete* design: 49 stitches,
the other parts of the motif are executed as reflections, start where indicated by the arrows

one quarter of the complete design

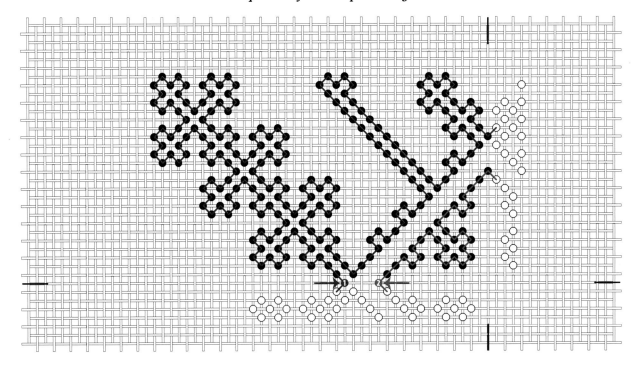

A few examples of "de sterrimentu" (framework) motifs

s'arenada • the pomegranate

design width: 51 stitches, height of **complete** design: 51 stitches,
the other half of the motif is executed as a reflection, start where indicated by the arrow

one half of the complete design

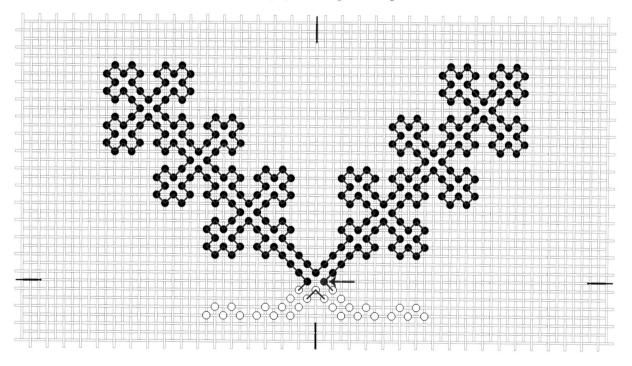

A few examples of "de sterrimentu" (framework) motifs

sa cadira • the chair

design width: 65 stitches, design height: 47 stitches, start where indicated by the arrows

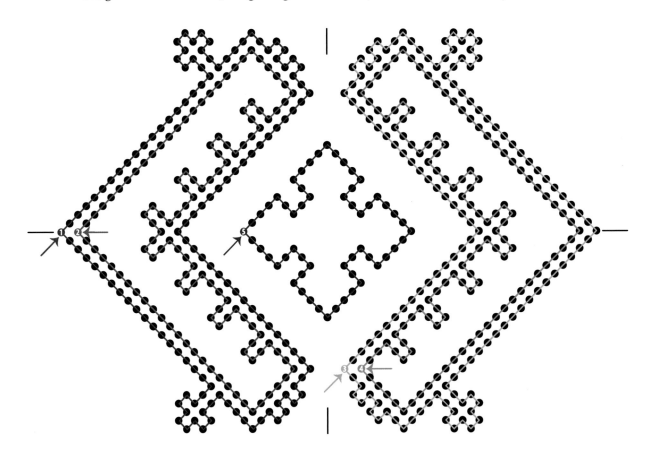

A few examples of "de sterrimentu" (framework) motifs

is caboniscus a copias • a pair of cockerels

width of **complete** design: 125 stitches, design height: 34 stitches,
the other half of the motif is executed as a reflection, start where indicated by the arrows

one half of the complete design

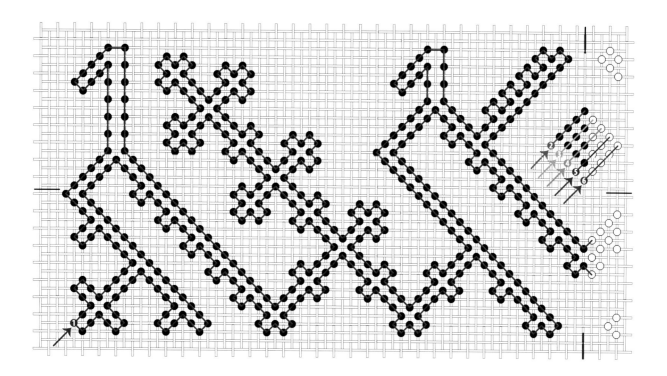

A few examples of "de prenimentu" (embellishment) motifs

su caboniscu • the cockerel

design width: 31 stitches, design height: 35 stitches, start where indicated by the arrow

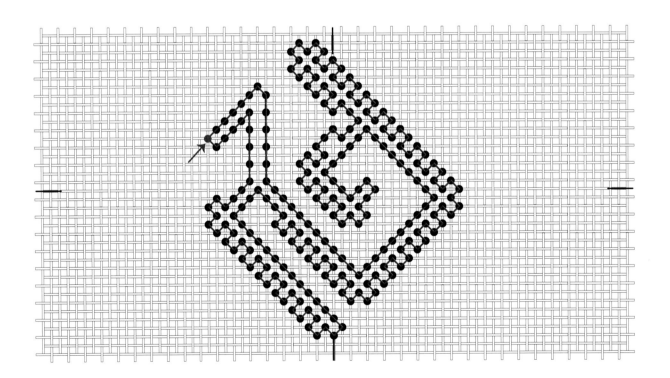

A few examples of "de prenimentu" (embellishment) motifs

su cuadrifòliu • the four leaf clover

design width: 19 stitches, design height: 19 stitches, start where indicated by the arrow

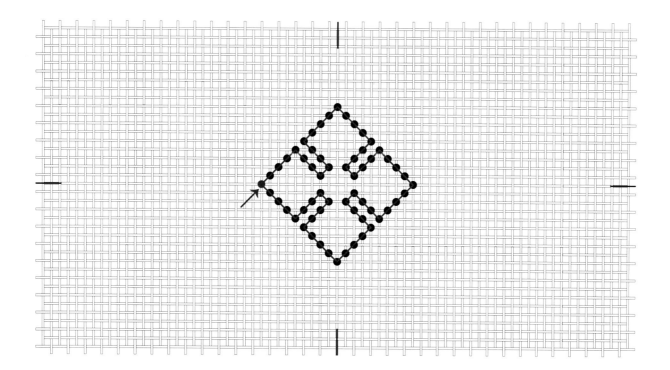

A few examples of "de prenimentu" (embellishment) motifs

su cuadrifòliu • the four leaf clover

design width: 27 stitches, design height: 27 stitches, start where indicated by the arrow

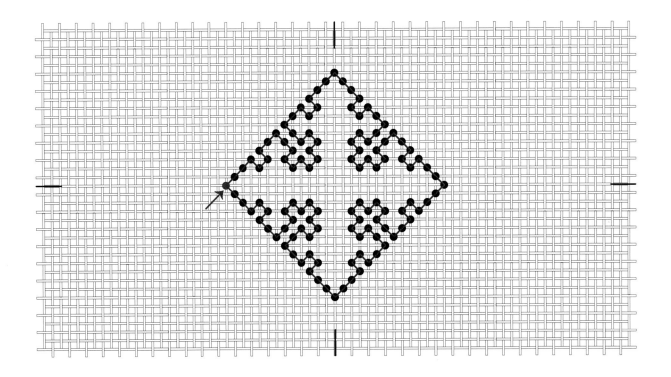

A few examples of "de prenimentu" (embellishment) motifs

sa menduledda • the almond

design width: 37 stitches, design height: 37 stitches, start where indicated by the arrows

A few examples of "de prenimentu" (embellishment) motifs

sa prama • the palm tree

design width: 69 stitches, design height: 28 stitches, start where indicated by the arrow

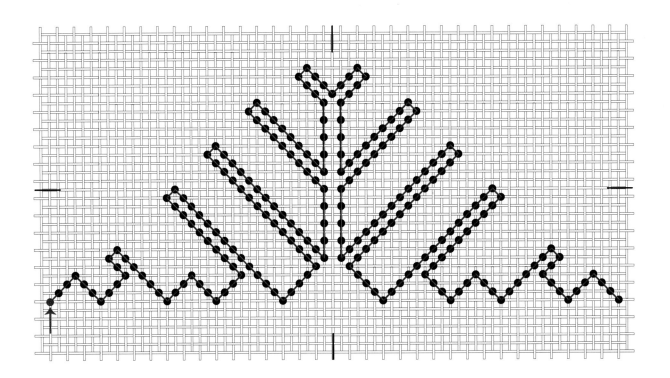

A few examples of "de prenimentu" (embellishment) motifs
sa prama • the palm tree
design width: 23 stitches, design height: 107 stitches, start where indicated by the arrow

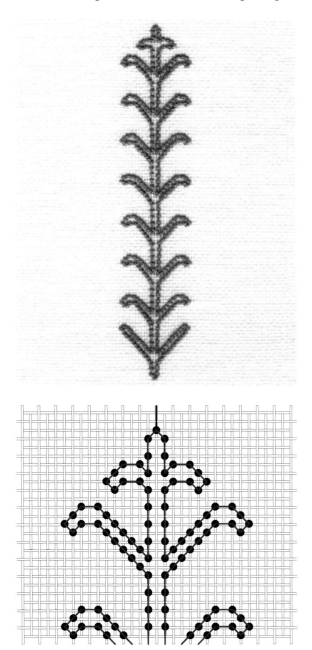

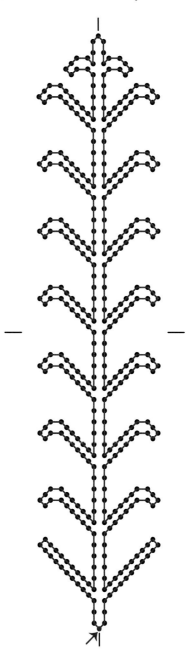

A few examples of simple motifs

is cerexias • the cherries

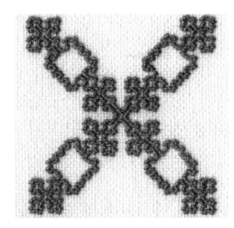

design width: 60 stitches, height of *complete* design: 60 stitches, start where indicated by the arrow, the other half of the motif is executed as a reflection
one half of the complete design

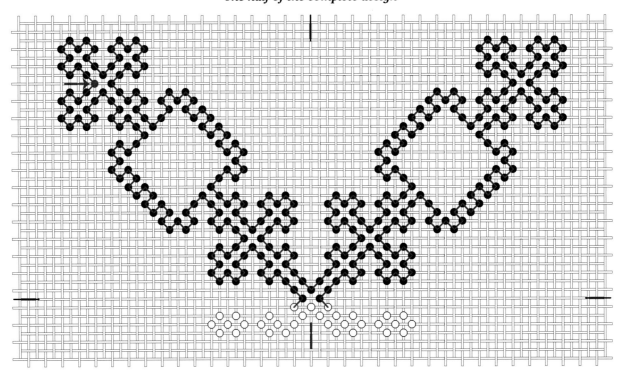

A few examples of simple motifs

su calixi picau • the hammered chalice

design width: 42 stitches, design height: 39 stitches, start where indicated by the arrows

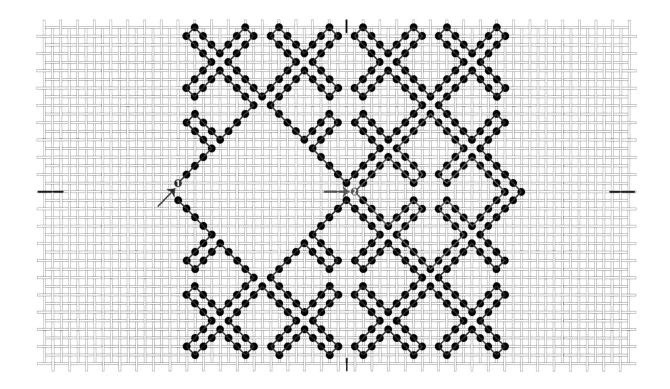

Projects

In this section we *propose a few "non traditional" projects to make with Sardinian Knot Stitch of increasing difficulty and complexity, but all are suitable for those who are approaching this kind of traditional Sardinian embroidery for the first time.*

For each project you will find a list of materials, the instructions and the pattern for the execution of the embroidery, and the instructions for assembly and finishing, complete with step-by-step photos which illustrate the various phases of the work.

The instructions and the patterns were written, drawn and stitched and errors were corrected along the way but due to the quirks of all handiwork, the photos of the work may not exactly match the patterns of the projects proposed.

You will find a:
- Biscornu: Sardinian Heart. Level of difficulty: beginner.
- Biscornu: Four Leaf Clover. Level of difficulty: intermediate.
- Bookmark: Cockerel. Level of difficulty: intermediate. There are also other patterns for making a bookmark with the motifs of "the rose" or "the crosses".
- Christmas Tree Decoration: Snowflake. Level of difficulty: intermediate. There are also another four patterns of snowflake designs.
- Lampshade: Level of difficulty: intermediate.
- Cushion: Level of difficulty: advanced.

Biscornu: Sardinian Heart

Level of difficulty: beginner. Dimensions of the finished work: approx. 7 x 7 cm

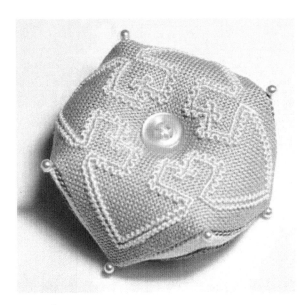

Requirements

- 28ct evenweave fabric: two squares measuring 12 cm per side
- Pearl cotton thread no. 12
- The fabric and thread colours can be chosen according to your taste and imagination *(model uses: 28ct Wichelt Jobelan fabric in Ivory with DMC pearl cotton no. 12, colour 223 thread and 28ct Zweigart Jazlyn fabric in English Rose with DMC pearl cotton no. 12, colour 712 thread)*
- Batting
- Beads *(model uses 3 mm Gutermann glass beads, colour: 1016)*
- Two buttons
- Two small squares of fabric to serve as reinforcement under the buttons
- Tapestry needle no. 24
- Beading needle
- Long darning needle

Embroidery and assembly instructions

Using basting thread, baste the horizontal and vertical centres on the fabric squares. As you can see from the pattern, the design is not perfectly centred (between the design and the border on two sides there are 7 fabric threads while on the remaining 2 sides there are only 6). Execute the embroidery following the instructions for Sardinian Knot Stitch. Embroider the external motif (red path) for the entire perimeter and then embroider the internal motif (blue path). Once finished the embroidery, using the same thread, execute the row of backstitches over two fabric threads at a distance of 6 fabric threads away from the embroidery on two sides and 7 on the remaining two sides (see pattern). This border will be used to assemble the biscornu. Execute the backstitch border on the second piece of fabric, paying attention that they are identical (in this case 39 backstitches per side). On the back side of the work at the centre of both pieces of fabric where the buttons will eventually go, pin one of the small squares of fabric for reinforcement. The fabric square should be slightly larger than the button. Fold a 1 cm seam allowance along the backstitched line toward the back side of the work. With right sides together, align the two fabric pieces along the backstitched line, matching the corner of one to the centre of one side of the other and execute an overcasting stitch into each backstitch, taking care not to catch the fabric underneath. Attach a bead at the corner, turn the work and continue. Work in this way until you meet up with where you started remembering to leave a small section unstitched in order to insert the batting. Fill the biscornu and close the opening with overcasting stitches. Using the long darning needle, attach the buttons on the top side and under side at the same time pulling your thread tightly to obtain the shape required. Secure the working thread by wrapping it around the central thread core under one button and then inserting the needle through the core. Bury the thread end inside the biscornu.

Biscornu Assembly

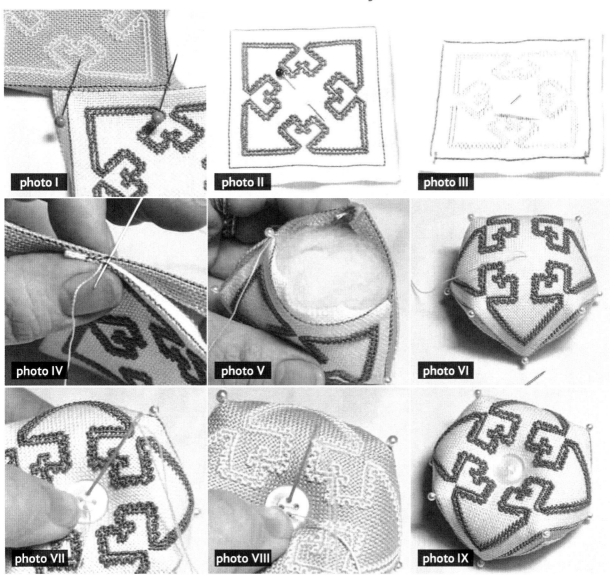

photo I

photo II

photo III

photo IV

photo V

photo VI

photo VII

photo VIII

photo IX

Su Coru • The Heart: Pattern

external square border: 39 x 39 backstitches embroidered over 2 fabric threads,
pattern: 65 x 65 stitches, start where indicated by the arrows

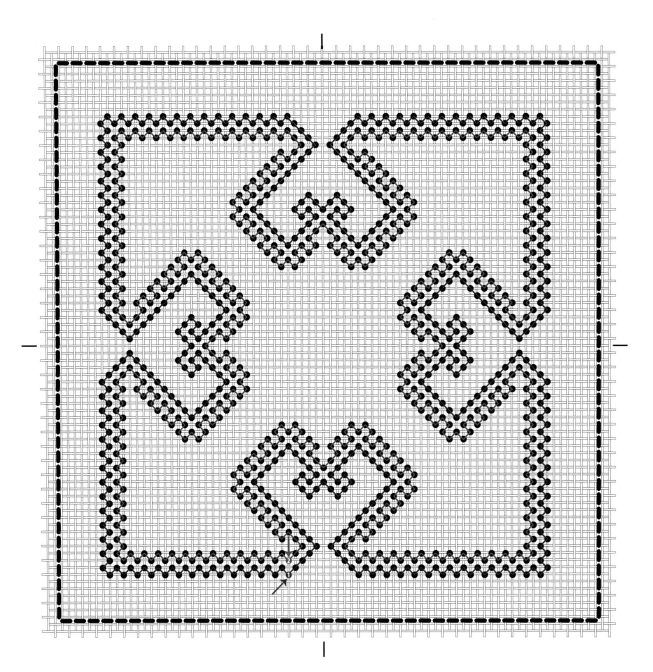

Biscornu: Four Leaf Clover

Level of difficulty: intermediate. Dimensions of the finished work: approx. 7 x 7 cm

Requirements

- 28ct evenweave fabric: two squares measuring 12 cm per side
- Pearl cotton thread no. 12
- The fabric and thread colours can be chosen according to your taste and imagination *(model uses: Sotema Assisi in Ocra [no. 15] fabric and DMC Retors d'Alsace no. 12, colour 920 thread)*
- Batting
- Two buttons
- Two small squares of fabric to serve as reinforcement under the buttons
- Tapestry needle no. 24
- Long darning needle

Embroidery and assembly instructions

Baste the horizontal and vertical centres on the fabric squares. Execute the embroidery following the instructions for Sardinian Knot Stitch.

Top side: start with the "isolated" motif in the top left corner (red path). Then the next motif (blue path) and the remaining "isolated" motifs (orange paths) in each corner. Do the central motifs (green paths) last. ***Bottom side:*** once finished the embroidery, using the same thread, execute the row of backstitches over two fabric threads (see pattern for spacing - note the bottom pattern has 10 fabric threads between the design and the border on two sides and 9 on the remaining two sides). Execute the backstitch border on the second piece of fabric, paying attention that they are identical. On the back side of the work at the centre of both pieces of fabric where the buttons will eventually go, pin one of the small squares of fabric for reinforcement. The fabric square should be slightly larger than the button. Fold back a 1 cm seam allowance and with right sides together, line up the two fabric pieces by matching the corner of one, to the centre of one side of the other and execute an overcasting stitch into each of the backstitches, taking care not to catch the fabric underneath. Arriving at the corner, turn the work and continue. Work in this way until you meet up with where you started remembering to leave a small section unstitched in order to insert the batting. Fill the biscornu and close the opening with overcasting stitches. Using the long darning needle, attach the buttons on the top side and underside at the same time pulling your thread tightly to obtain the shape required. Finish the working thread by wrapping it around the central thread core under one button and then inserting the needle through the core. Bury the thread end inside the biscornu.

Su Cuadrifòlliu • The Four Leaf Clover: Pattern, top square

external square border: 39 x 39 backstitches embroidered over 2 fabric threads
pattern: 77 x 77 stitches, start where indicated by the arrows

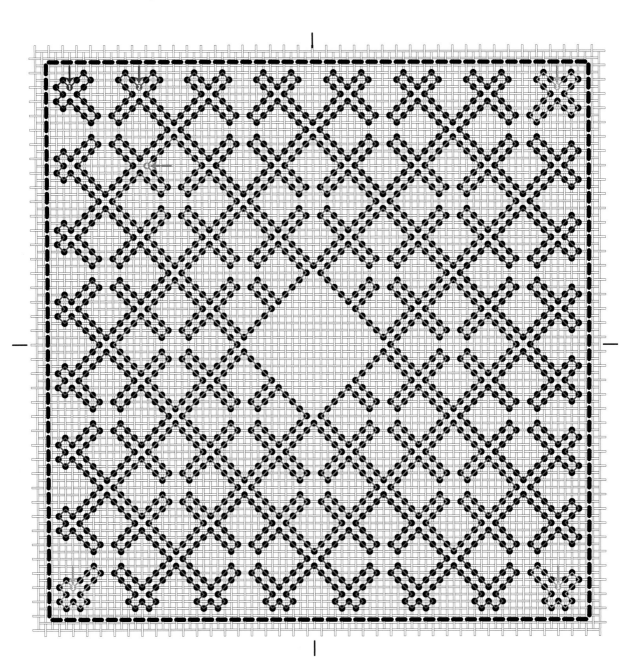

Su Cuadrifòlliu • The Four Leaf Clover: Pattern, bottom square

external square border: 39 x 39 backstitches embroidered over 2 fabric threads
pattern: 59 x 59 stitches, start where indicated by the arrow

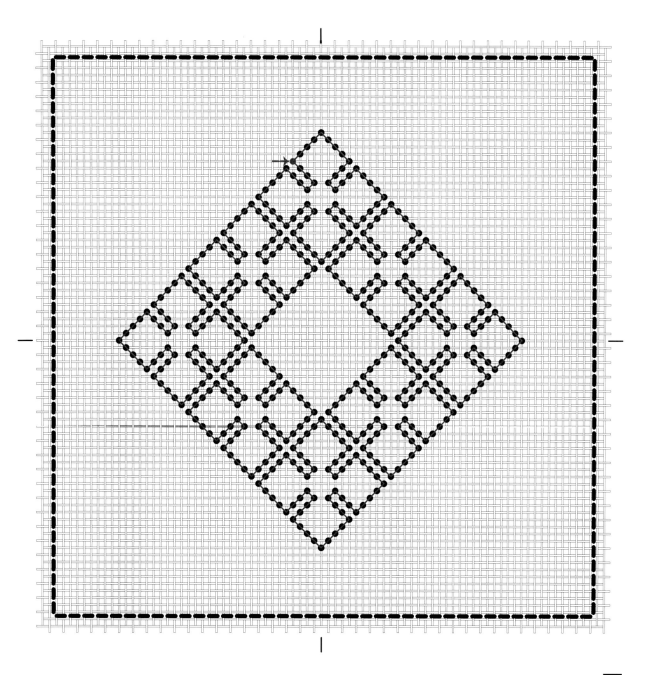

Su Caboniscu • The Cockerel

S'Arrosa • The Rose

Is Gruxittas • The Crosses

For all bookmarks: *external border: long sides: 60 backstitches embroidered over 3 fabric threads*
top sides: 7 backstitches embroidered over 3 fabric threads
tip: 1 backstitch embroidered over 3 fabric threads
bottom: 15 backstitches embroidered over 3 fabric threads

Bookmark: Cockerel

Level of difficulty: intermediate. Dimensions of the finished work: approx. 4 x 17.5 cm

Requirements

- 28ct evenweave fabric: two rectangles measuring 6 x 20 cm
- Pearl cotton thread no. 12 *(model uses: Anchor Ritorto Fiorentino no. 12, colours 108 and 111 thread)*
- A piece of felt, fleece or fusible interfacing measuring approximately 4 x 17.5 cm
- Tapestry needle no. 24

Embroidery and assembly instructions

Cut two 6 x 20 cm rectangles of fabric.

Following the pattern, at a distance of approximately 1 cm from the edge of the fabric, execute a backstitch row over 3 fabric threads making one of the short sides into the point.

Embroider one or both rectangles with the motif in Sardinian Knot Stitch.

On the wrong side of one rectangle, inside the backstitch line baste a piece of felt which you have cut to the appropriate dimensions.

underneath. If desired, the overcasting can be done in a thread of contrasting colour.

Remove the basting. You can embellish the upper part of the bookmark with a series of buttonhole stitch arcs with picots following the instructional photo sequence which follows.

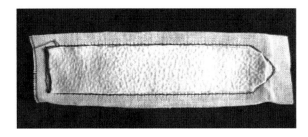

After having folded a 1 cm seam allowance to the back side of the work, join the two rectangles together executing an overcasting stitch into each backstitch taking care not to catch the fabric

Buttonhole Stitch Arcs with Picot:

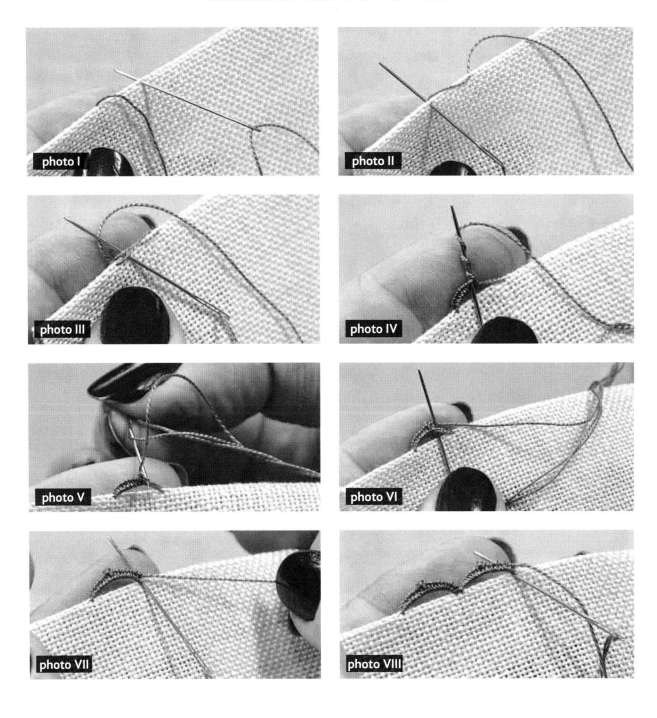

Su Caboniscu • The Cockerel: Pattern
motif: 40 x 188 stitches, start where indicated by the arrows

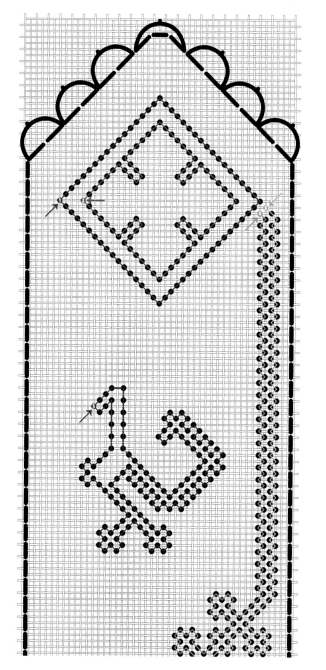 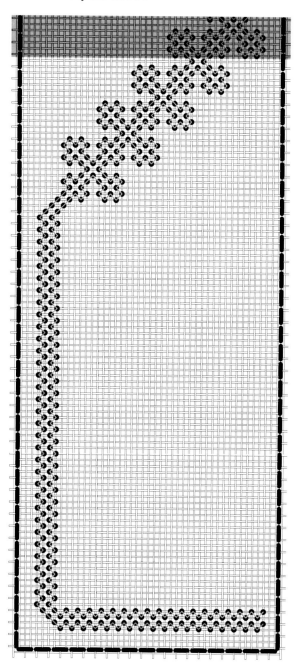

S'Arrosa • The Rose: Pattern

motif: 15 x 115 stitches, start where indicated by the arrows

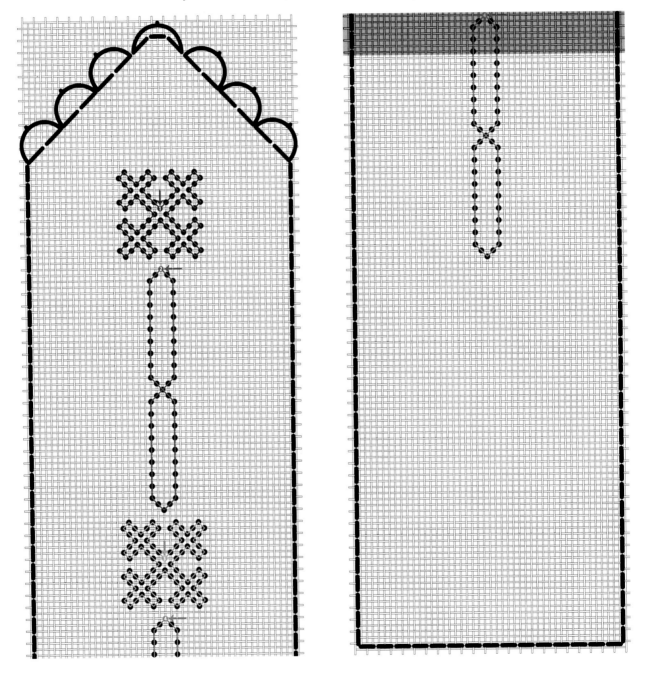

Is Gruxittasa • The Crosses: Pattern

motif: 41 x 185 stitches, start where indicated by the arrows

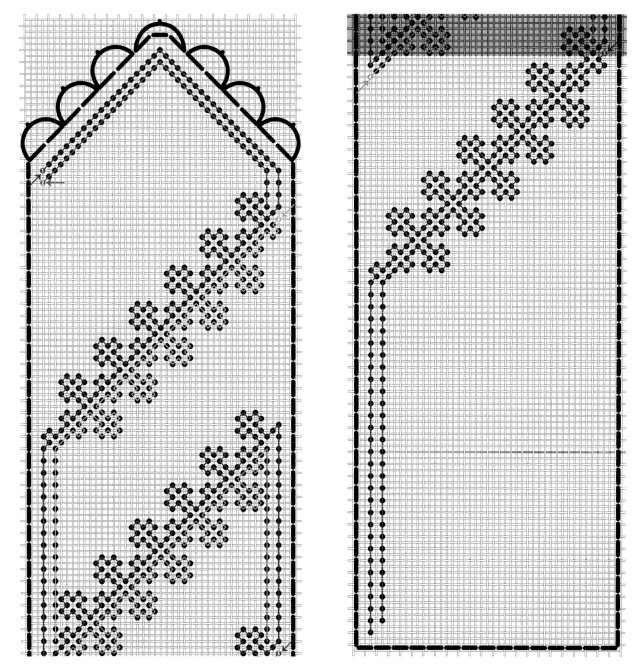

Christmas Tree Decoration: Snowflake

Level of difficulty: intermediate. Dimensions of the finished work: approx. 8 x 8 cm

Requirements
- 28ct evenweave fabric: two squares measuring 10 cm per side
- Pearl cotton thread no. 8
- The fabric and thread colours can be chosen according to your taste and imagination (*model uses: Bellora linen in Ecru and Anchor Ritorto Fiorentino no. 8, colour 46 thread*)
- Batting
- Tapestry needle no. 24
- Long darning needle
- A rectangle of cardboard 2.5 cm longer than the length you would like your tassel

Embroidery and assembly instructions

First of all, mark the horizontal and vertical centers of the area to be embroidered with a running stitch using a basting thread. Execute the embroidery following the patterns provided and the instructions for Sardinian Knot Stitch. Once the embroidery is finished, using the same thread, work a row of backstitches over two fabric threads at a distance of 1 cm from the edge of the fabric on all four sides of both fabric squares paying attention that all sides are identical. These borders will be used to assemble the two sides of the decoration. Fold a seam allowance of 1 cm towards the back side of the work and join the two squares together with an overcasting stitch into each backstitch paying attention not to catch the fabric underneath. Leave a small opening in order to insert the batting. Fill the decoration then overcast the opening closed. Attach the tassel and the hanger loop.

Tassel construction

Wrap the thread around the cardboard until it is the desired density. Loosely tie a long thread around the upper end of the cardboard passing underneath the wrapped thread. Cut the wrapped threads along the bottom edge of the cardboard using a large pair of scissors. Tie a knot at the top of the threads and create the head of the tassel by wrapping a thread around the "neck" as shown. Trim the ends of the tassel so that all of the fringe is the same length. Attach it to the embroidery as shown. Create the hanger loop.

Decoration Assembly and Tassel Construction

photo I

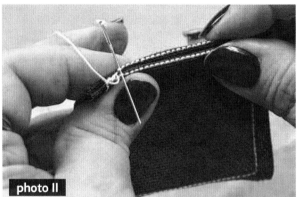

photo II

photo III

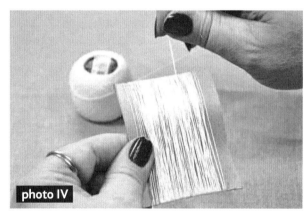

photo IV

photo V

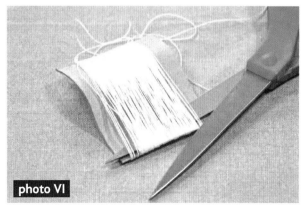

photo VI

Decoration Assembly and Tassel Construction - continued

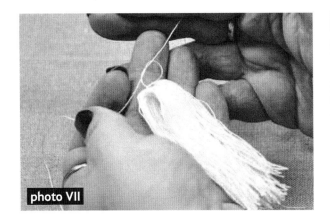

photo VII

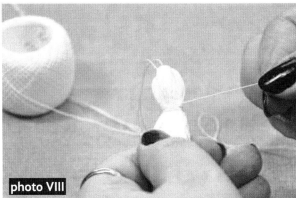

photo VIII

photo IX

photo X

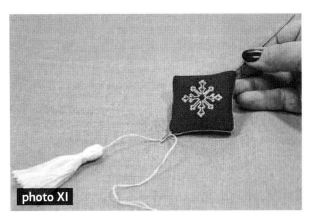

photo XI

photo XII

Snowflake: Pattern

pattern: 53 x 53 stitches, start where indicated by the arrow

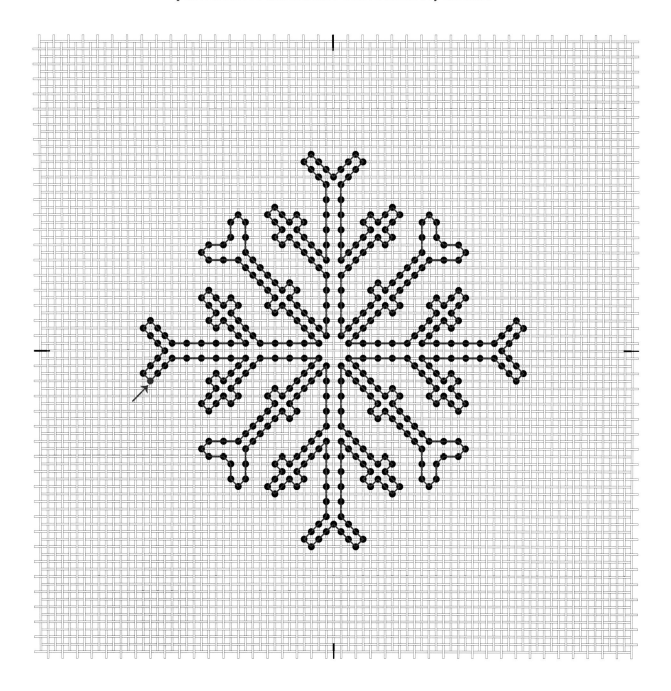

More Designs

the fabric and thread colours can be chosen according to your taste and imagination

Snowflake 2

Snowflake 3

Snowflake 4

Snowflake 5

Snowflake 2: Pattern

pattern: 79 x 79 stitches, start where indicated by the arrows

Snowflake 3: Pattern
pattern: 47 x 47 stitches,
start where indicated by the arrow

Snowflake 4: Pattern
pattern: 37 x 37 stitches,
start where indicated by the arrow

Snowflake 5: Pattern

pattern: 67 x 67 stitches, start where indicated by the arrows

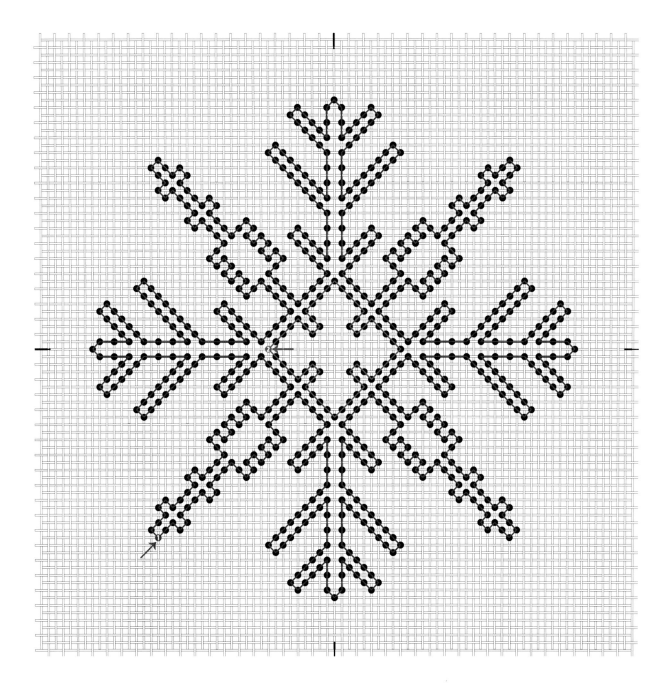

Lampshade

Level of difficulty: intermediate. Dimensions of the finished work: approx. 49 x 16 cm

Requirements

- 28ct evenweave fabric: 20 x 53 cm
- Pearl cotton thread no. 12
- 2.20 m of white trimming approximately 1.5 cm in height
- The fabric and thread colours can be chosen according to your taste and imagination *(model uses: 28ct white evenweave fabric and Anchor Ritorto Fiorentino no. 12, colour 891 thread)*
- Tapestry needle no. 24
- White sewing cotton thread
- Hot glue gun
- Lampshade cylinder: height 16 cm; diameter 15.5 cm; circumference approximately 49 cm
- clothespins

Embroidery instructions

Finish the edges of the fabric on a sewing machine. Baste the central lines. Embroider the central motif making sure to align the centre of the motif to the centre of the fabric. Follow the pattern for the stitching sequence. At a distance of 2 cm from the edge of the fabric embroider the border motif, noting that at the top and bottom centre of the border pattern where it is directly above and below the points of the center motif, there are only three stitches instead of four. Reproduce the other parts of the border motif as a reflection of the pattern provided.

Lampshade assembly

Wash and iron on the back side of the work using a thick towel as a base so as not to flatten the embroidery. With right sides together, baste the two short sides together and check that the fabric fits over the lampshade "cylinder". Sew over the basting with a sewing machine and press the seam open. Turn the work right side out and fit the fabric over the lampshade folding the upper and lower edges over the openings using the 2 cm allowance. Keeping the fabric taut, glue the two folded edges inside the lampshade and glue the trimming over the unfinished edges. Hold in place with the clothespins until the glue is completely dry.

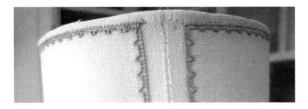

View of rear stitching.

Lampshade: Pattern

*central motif design: 153 x 153 stitches, **borders excluded,***
start where indicated by the arrows

one quarter of the central design

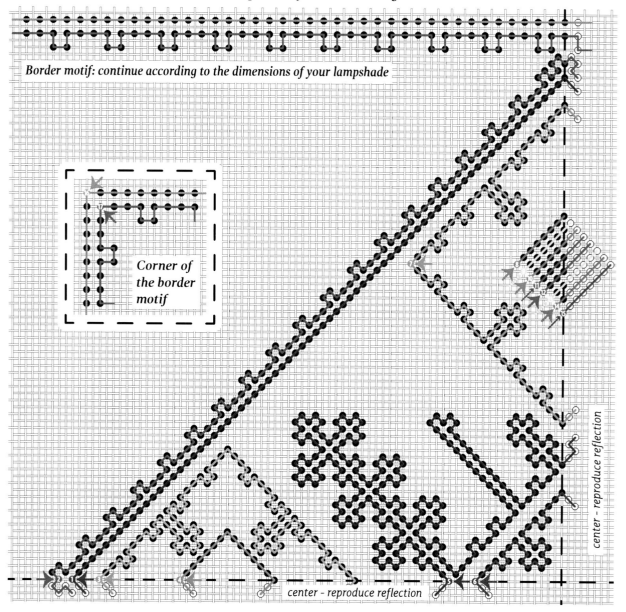

Border motif: continue according to the dimensions of your lampshade

*Corner of
the border
motif*

center - reproduce reflection

center - reproduce reflection

Cushion

Level of difficulty: advanced. Dimensions of the finished work: approx. 50 x 50 cm

Requirements

• 28ct evenweave fabric: one square 52 x 52 cm for the embroidery on the front, two rectangles 27 x 52 cm for the back
• Pearl cotton thread no. 12
• The fabric and thread colours can be chosen according to your taste and imagination *(model uses: Sotema Assisi colour Rosa Scuro [no. 171] and Anchor Ritorto Fiorentino no. 12, colour bianco thread)*
• Tapestry needle no. 24
• Fringe trimming approximately 220 cm
• Pink zipper approximately 45 cm
• Batting

Embroidery instructions

First of all, mark the horizontal and vertical centers of the area to be embroidered with a running stitch using a basting thread.

Execute all of the embroidery following the patterns provided and the instructions for Sardinian Knot Stitch.

Note that due to the large dimensions of the complete pattern for the cushion, it has been divided over several pages.

To facilitate the work, we recommend making a working copy and pasting the sections together, overlapping them along the shaded areas.

Once the working copies are assembled you can then have mirror images made to follow for the remaining areas.

Cushion assembly

For the cushion back: with right sides together, sew the long side of the two rectangles of fabric together remembering to leave an opening at the centre for the zipper. Use a seam allowance of 1 cm from the edge of the fabric for about 5 cm at the two ends.

Position the zipper and baste it into place, then sew it by hand or machine, using the appropriate foot (if applicable), on the right side.

You should now have a square of fabric equal in dimension to that of the piece with the embroidery for the front.

Baste the fringe trimming into place on one of the squares of fabric with the fringe toward the inside. Place the right sides of the two fabric squares together and baste.

Sewing on the wrong side, join all four sides of the squares together.

Turn the work right sides out, wash and iron on the back side using a thick towel as a base so as not to flatten the embroidery. Insert the batting.

Cushion: Pattern

complete dimensions of the entire frame motif: 496 x 496 stitches, approximately 45 cm,
one quarter of the complete design

centre - reproduce reflection

centre - reproduce reflection

Cushion: Pattern

complete dimensions of the entire frame motif: 496 x 496 stitches, approximately 45 cm,
detail: the space between the frame motif and the central motif

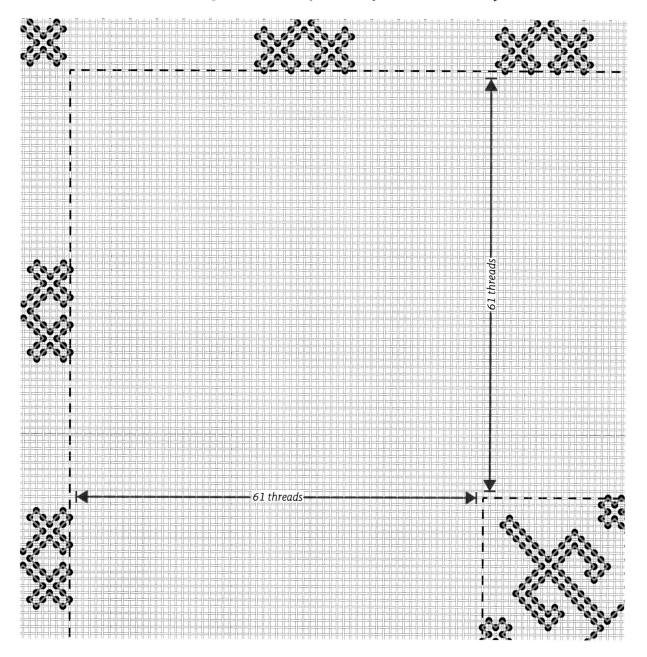

Cushion: Pattern - Central Area

complete dimensions of the entire central motif: : 208 x 208 stitches, approximately 19 cm,
start where indicated by the arrows · **one quarter of the central pattern**

Cushion: Pattern - Top left corner of the Frame

complete dimensions of the entire frame motif: 496 x 496 stitches, approximately 45 cm,
start where indicated by the arrows

Cushion: Pattern - Top horizontal band of the Frame (continued from corner pg. 65)

complete dimensions of the entire frame motif: 496 x 496 stitches, approximately 45 cm,
start where indicated by the arrows

Cushion: Pattern - Top horizontal band of the Frame (continued)

complete dimensions of the entire frame motif: 496 x 496 stitches, approximately 45 cm, start where indicated by the arrows

Cushion: Pattern - Left vertical band of the Frame (continued from corner pg. 65)

complete dimensions of the entire frame motif: 496 x 496 stitches, approximately 45 cm,
start where indicated by the arrows

Cushion: Pattern - Left vertical band of the Frame (continued)

*complete dimensions of the entire frame motif: 496 x 496 stitches, approximately 45 cm,
start where indicated by the arrows*

centre - reproduce reflection

Stitching Sequence Legend

Due to lack of *space, we were sometimes forced to reduce the patterns. It was often difficult to clearly identify the numbers and colours of the stitching sequences so we thought we would list them on this page in a size which is easier to read.*

Bibliography

Addis, prof. Ovidio – *Trilogia teuladina: Teulada tra storia e leggenda,* Supplement to no. 5 of "Il Nuovo Solco" Poesia, dramma e storia della toponomastica sarda, Tuerra – S. Isidoro – Pere Portas, (no date). http://users.libero.it/efisio.desogus/teulada.htm

Culurgioni, prof.ssa Quintina – *Su Punt'e Nù e su Punt'a Brodu,* publication edited by the Commune of Teulada, Carbonia, (no date).

Davanzo Poli, prof.ssa Doretta – *Tessuti: Tradizione e innovazione della tessitura in Sardegna,* Chapter: Tessitura come linguaggio: decorazione e simboli, edited by Ilisso Edizioni, Nuoro, 2006.

Mulas, prof.ssa Gisella – *Le botteghe dei tessuti tradizionali ed il costume sardo* publication edited by the Commune of Teulada, Carbonia, 2010.

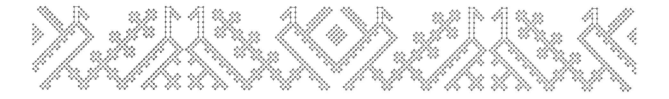

Made in the USA
Middletown, DE
30 September 2023

39831438R00044